FROM THE HOUSE OF DAVID

Charles B. Carson

Thank you, Enjoy

Chuck Carson

i

From the House of David — Book 1 by Charles B. Carson
Copyright © 2021. All rights reserved.

Published by Pen It! Publications, LLC in the U.S.A.
812-371-4128   www.penitpublications.com

ISBN: 978-1-63984-103-5
Cover Design by Donna Cook
Edited by Jen Selinsky

Happy Christmas, Marley!
We love you,
Uncle Danny and
Aunt Martina

Table of Contents

Matthew 1; 18-23 - 24-25
Luke 2: 1-5
Matthew 2; 13-23
Luke 2; 41-50
Isayah;11, 1

BIRTH OF JOSEPH

Bethlehem

My name is Joseph. Rachel, my mama, told me my beginning was a little different from my siblings'. Being the middle child, I felt suppressed by my older brothers; even my younger brothers joined in until I was eight. I felt like the forgotten child most of the time. My siblings' bullying was a form of attention I unfortunately grew used to. My faith, and reading scripture, gave me some comfort.

The sun was setting in the Western horizon, darkness was ascending quickly. My papa, Jacob, was wearing his favorite worn-out work tunic, draped to his knees, and sandals. He was busy in the stable, cleaning stalls, feeding, and watering our only milk cow, a couple goats, a few sheep, and a donkey. The stench of animal dung radiated in the air from a collective pile fermenting a short distance from the stable. Dung was utilized for fertilizer for our garden.

As Jacob was finishing, an incredible light appeared at the stable entrance, silhouetting; a figure began to materialize, garbed in a white flowing robe.

Papa threw up his hands to shade the glare from his eyes, and he hunched in fear.

"*Jacob,*" the figure with a deep voice called, "*Do not be afraid, I am the Angel, Gabriel, with a message from the Lord Almighty. Rachel is delivering your son. The Lord has decreed that you shall name the baby Joseph and he will be remembered eternally for his Lord's service. Go now and meet your son.*"

Then as quickly as he appeared, he vanished.

Papa stood in awe, for several minutes, shaking in disbelief and shock.

***

Sarah, Mama's midwife, attended to Mama as the other ladies were comforting her, soothing her face with a cool, wet towel.

One lady was attentively massaging Rachel's belly with olive oil, widely used to reduce the intensity of contractions during labor.

Sarah was surprised how quickly Rachel was progressing. "Push, Rachel, push. Your baby is in a hurry to greet the world."

Following my delivery, Mama collapsed upon the bed.

Sarah handed me to another lady, who cleaned and rubbed me with salt then olive oil. Afterwards, she swaddled me in a traditional Hebrew wool blanket. I was crying loudly. She handed me back to Mama directly after Mama had been cleaned and redressed.

"You have done well, Rachel," Sarah praised Mother. "You have another healthy son."

My brother, Asa, six, listening intently to everything from the other room, rushed outdoors.

***

"My dear Lord, did I really experience this?" my father, Jacob, said to himself, "Did You really send me an angel?"

Asa entered the stable, clothed in his hand-me down, woven, flaxen tunic and barefoot. "Papa, Papa, come quick!" he yelled. Asa's chest was heaving from running.

Papa's hands instinctively grasped his chest in startled fear, shouting, "AAAHHH!"

"Asa, calm down," Papa said, recovering. He jumped up and placed both his hands upon Asa's shoulders until Asa relaxed and caught his breath. "A terrible fright you nearly gave me, child!" he exclaimed, trying to slow down his pulse. "What is so urgent?"

"Mama has had the baby, and it's a boy," he announced, excitedly.

"Praise to The Almighty," Father shouted. "Are Mama and the child healthy?"

"Yes, Papa. I was not permitted to enter, but I could hear the baby crying and I heard Mama's voice. The ladies said both are doing well," he replied.

Now, Jacob truly believed. Papa exited the stable, rounded the corner, and entered the home

3

with Asa in tow. Normally, the aroma of baking bread, cooking, and clamor of shuffling of feet on the dirt floor from the process of domestic activities was apparent. Not today.

Papa reached the dark bedroom doorway, with Asa on his heels, not wishing to miss anything.

My older brother, Jesse, had gone fishing and had missed all the excitement.

Mama was recovering in bed.

Several ladies were standing around chatting. They went silent, turned, and greeted him when he arrived.

"Good evening, ladies," Papa greeted them, still a little shaken. "Thank you all for your help. Are Rachel and the child doing well?"

"Good evening, Jacob," they all replied in unison.

Sarah answered for the rest. "Rachel is doing fine, and you both have another beautiful baby boy, Jacob." Then, she asked, "What name have you chosen?" They were all wondering about that. Sarah was just the boldest to inquire.

"You are all aware his name will be announced during the Brit Milah circumcision ceremony in eight days," he said, smiling, dashing their hopes for an early declaration.

***

Later that evening, after all the ladies had left, Papa shared privately with Mama about Gabriel's visit.

"Rachel, please do not be alarmed, but I thought I lost my mind earlier," Jacob began. "An Angel, Gabriel, appeared to me, in our stable, with a message from The Almighty. He told me you were to have a boy and his name was to be Joseph. Gabriel also told me Joseph would be forever remembered for doing great things for The Almighty, in his lifetime."

"Jacob, have you been into the altar wine, again?" Rachael asked, frowning, wondering if Jacob had dreamed it.

"No, Rachel, this really happened."

Mama looked at Papa with an expression of great concern on her face. As Mama studied his features, she realized Papa was serious, and he shook a little.

"Jacob," she stated, "I have never had a reason to doubt you before, and I do not doubt you now. It shall be as proclaimed."

***

My brother, Jesse, had returned from fishing and was excited about the news of a new brother.

"Shush," Jesse put a finger up to his lips and suggested putting their ears to the wall adjoining their parents' bedroom. "Let's listen and hear what Papa and Mama are saying."

Jesse's happy facial expression changed drastically into anger when overhearing his father's revelation.

"What does that mean," Asa asked Jesse?

"It means he's special or something and they're going to love him more; that's what it means," Jesse sneered in anguish.

With tears in his eyes and pain in his voice, he ran from the house and into the night. I truly believe an evil entity placed resentment into Jesse's heart with malice toward me. Jesse's influence enviably affected my other siblings.

***

On the eighth day, as per Jewish belief, was the Brit Milah ceremony. I was circumcised and my name was divulged. Selecting Joseph drew some criticism from some of the elders, but Father stood his ground, and my name remained.

My brother, Jesse, overheard the elders as they questioned naming me Joseph because this was not a past family name. Change in any form was unpopular. It was just another reason for him to hate me more.

JOSEPH, THE APPRENTICESHIP

A few years went by and three more brothers were added to the family. Life was not always stressful. We had some good times, too. We spent hours playing with kick balls; hand-woven balls crafted from reeds and stuffed with goat hair and leaves. It was great fun. A fashion of dodgeball, introduced by the Roman children over the years, was fun, but the game could get intense and painful. Summer months could generate a suffocating atmosphere in our sleeping room without a window for ventilation.

"Mama and Papa, it is too hot to sleep in our room. Could we sleep on the roof?"

"Of course, you all may," they replied, "Be careful climbing the ladder and don't fall."

"We'll be careful," we all said in unison upon rushing out the door.

At night, cool breezes blew over the house, gentling swaying the sod grass blades. The sod made for comfortable sleeping mats. Listening to the crickets chirping, the airstream blowing through the trees, frogs croaking, and distant owls calling, serenaded us to sleep for many peaceful nights. Then, there were other times that were more stressful.

One night, an idea, as a prank, entered Jesse's mind to push me off the roof.

I landed on soft moss growing beside our house. I was not injured, but I no longer slept aloft.

"Hey, Josey," Jesse would taunt me while meditating with my other brothers in gang mode. I accepted that my younger brothers were too young to really understand. "Why are you so special? Aren't we as good as you? The Rabbi says you are nothing special. So do the elders. Even the village kids do not see why you are so different. How come you pray all the time? Are you a holy boy or something?"

If I did not respond, the aggression amplified. My older brothers would push and shove me when I was alone. I knew my younger brothers partook out of fear and peer pressure. When I had had enough, I tried to fight back, but I was so much smaller, and I could not stand a chance; not against all five; therefore, bruises ensued.

Violent punching and kicking upon me were often common forms of their retaliation. Several other accidents occurred, but without any severe reaction.

Later in in life, thinking back, I acknowledged I was being divinely protected from any real permanent harm. Mama would intervene when she came upon a scuffle and would rescue me, driving the boys away.

"You boys leave Joseph alone," she would scold them. "He has done nothing to you. I am going to tell your father when he gets home," she warned.

Eventually, they became resourcefully careful not to leave any visible bruises beyond my clothing seams when encounters incurred. Punishment from previous encounters made Jesse more vigilant and stealthier. Avoiding them took planned ingenuity.

"You tell anyone," Jesse warned me, "and it will be worse next time."

I loved to create things from discarded wood I found. I taught myself, and with some guidance from my father, to design and construct rugged doll furniture, toys for neighborhood children, and household utensils for my mother. Papa brought home some carving tools and knives from the market when available and tried to pass on what little knowledge and skill he had.

We would spend hours together talking. I would sneak away with my wood scraps whenever possible. Whenever my brothers got the opportunity to find one of my creations, they would destroy or burn them out of fun or spite. I became exceptionally good at hiding my work. Sometimes, Papa would take some of my items to market and sell them. That made me so proud.

**

Early one morning while I was busy carving another kitchen tool for Mama, Papa and Mama approached me, accompanied by an unfamiliar man.

"Joseph, your mama and I have some exciting news. I was in the market this morning and met Elon," he said, introducing the stranger. "Elon is a well-known traveling Artesian and carpenter. He was admiring some of the items you made and was surprised you are only eight when I told him they were crafted by you. While we talked, Elon said he had been considering an apprentice and wondered if you might be interested. You would enrich your craft in woodworking and have the good fortune to travel."

I was surprised and asked, with fear and tears in my eyes, "Papa, have I done something wrong that you want to send me away?"

"Oh, no, my son, you are very talented," Father assured me, placing his hands on my shoulders and gently squeezing.

I winced a little from a recently inflicted bruise.

"Elon can develop your skill; he can teach you more than I ever could. Elon is widowed and has no children. He has promised to keep you safe and train you as his own. Wouldn't you like to increase your knowledge and grow in a trade you love? Are you not looking forward to new adventures?"

"Yes, Papa, I want to make you both proud and become the best craftsman in the world," I replied, becoming a little more at ease at the thought and opportunity. "I just don't want to leave you and Mama."

"I understand, Joseph. You are only eight, and it breaks our hearts to see you go, but it warms them at the same time. We will miss you terribly and will think of you every time we view one of Mama's utensils or a stool you made. I also am aware of the difficulties you have with your brothers. I am not always here to protect you. You have shown such promise in your artistry. This is your chance to be safe and learn more than I could ever teach you. Your mother and I will always be proud of you. Never doubt that."

I cried, uncontrollably, as we were leaving. I ran back and gave both my parents hugs and kisses, promising I would visit when we were in the area again. I heard Jesse mumble, "Good riddance."

"You will regret the way you treated me!" I shouted to my brother's contemptible sendoff. "In time, I will forgive you all."

Jesse sneered and shook his head in disgust.

My parents had wished me the best, but they never dreamed they would not see me again. Nor could they have known the prophecy of a carpenter was being fulfilled.

JOSEPH'S CAREER

I loved being with Elon. My thoughts of home gradually melted away.

"Joseph," Elon, would coach me, "we travel extensively. To become invaluable, we must know not only our craft, but we must also converse in the languages of the clients we encounter. This I will teach you."

"Yes, Master. I will learn everything you have to offer."

"I know you will, Joseph," he replied, smiling.

I learned other related talents such as masonry and architecture. I refined my knowledge and talent to design projects that would not only be beautiful but would endure for decades and be admired by everyone who viewed them.

As we traveled, I learned to speak and write conversational Aramaic, Greek, Latin, Egyptian, as well as some Arabic. My skill in building and carpentry became my passion. I absorbed all the tricks of the trade. I learned the different types and species of trees, and which were the best to be utilized for which project, depending on what was available in the area.

***

Elon addressed me one day, frowning. "Joseph, I have some disturbing news I have just received by messenger. Both of your parents have gone to be with Jehovah. Please, accept my sincerest condolences."

I was in severe shock. I wanted to go to see where they had been laid to rest, but we were so far away. Tears traveled down my cheeks in grief. I would never see them again.

"I promised to see them when we were near. I broke my promise," I cried, heartbroken, falling to my knees.

"You broke no promise, Joseph," Elon said, comforting me. "We have not been in the area for over five years for you to abide by that promise. I know they understood and were assured you were safe and happy and doing what you loved to do."

'Do you really think so, Master?" I asked, raising my head and peering into Elon's eyes.

"I am sure of it. You have nothing to regret. You are living the life they prayed you would have. Find solace in that," Elon assured me.

Shortly thereafter, Elon did something I never anticipated, he legally adopted me and made me his legal heir. I was so humbled by this honoring gesture.

***

Several wonderful years had elapsed when Elon unexpectedly perished from an unknown illness. On his death bed, Elon gave me his final blessing, witnessed by several close friends. This ancient Hebrew blessing empowered the eldest son with inheritance rights and entitlements. It also included authority over his mother and younger siblings. Not receiving a father's blessing was considered a curse.

***

After a mourning period, I continued developing the business and gained a reputation as an excellent Artisan. I was a master builder, mason, carver, and, of course, a carpenter. I created everything I could visualize with the artistry few could match. Working with wood would always be my first love, after the Lord.

***

I was nearing three decades when I was commissioned by a wealthy client, Amman, in the city of Nazareth. Amman had viewed a project I had completed for an associate friend of his from Jerusalem. Amman was so impressed with the skill and precision I possessed he retained me to build an elaborate dining area addition to his permanent residence.

The project progressed nicely. I hired local workmen to assist. I listened to any input and made alternative suggestions from Amman's specifications or preferences.

***

After several months, the dining hall was completed. While I was implementing the finishing touches, Amman invited me to a formal banquet to dedicate Amman's pride and joy, which included family, friends, and colleagues, before I took my leave. Inviting a builder to a diplomatic event was a great honor. It could potentially generate new prospective clientele.

After introductions, and exchanging pleasantries, I took advantage of the event and gave detailed design strategies for my work. Step by step construction explanations and ideas appeared to have impressed them all. It appeared I would be busy indefinitely.

"Joseph, pardon me, I would like to pull you away for a moment, if you wouldn't mind. May I introduce you to my wife and daughters?" Amman gently pulled me aside for a moment to officially meet his family; I had seen them all during the building process from a distance.

I graciously greeted them all. His three beautiful daughters were stairsteps of each other, ranging from ages of five to around fifteen. Being shy around women, I addressed the eldest daughter.

"Forgive me, miss, but I have met so many people, I seem to have forgotten your name." She caught my eye as soon as I had entered the room.

"Apology accepted; my name is Melcha, kind sir," she answered. Then, with a hint of sarcasm, she added, "Obviously, your memory is quite short. Do you forget your workers' names that quickly?" she asked, tilting her head, expressing a look of disdain while smiling.

Taken aback, both her parents looked aghast.

"Melcha!" her father reprimanded her, loudly. "We do not treat guests in this home in that manner. Apologize immediately!"

Melcha cowered and backed away in fright.

"That is quite all right, sir. Your daughter has spirit. I deserved that for my temporary lapse of memory," I addressed Amman.

Turning back to Melcha, I continued. "Forgive me again, Miss Melcha, no worker could ever resemble anything quite as exquisite as you, no matter the duration of my acquaintance. My memory loss is only matched by your insolence. I assure you, it will never happen again," I responded with a twinkle in my eye.

Melcha was rattled by my response. Her eyes burned with anger, and she blushed with embarrassment, as well.

We stared at each other, momentarily, our eyes never diverting from each other but turning softer.

Both her parents smiled.

Melcha had met her match, and a mutual attraction was obvious.

"She's hooked," her mother relayed to her husband, "and so is he."

***

During the next year, Melcha and I spent more time together, getting acquainted during our courtship. We were married a year later, to Amman and his wife's approval.

***

Melcha and I created a happy life and raised six children together, four boys, and two girls. In time, my knowledge of the scriptures and wisdom enabled me to be appointed as a Priest of the Temple of the Lord. I helped the poor and helpless whenever I could.

***

When the boys became of age, around the same age or a little older than in my youth, I took them to train in my craft, similar to what my master had done with me. I didn't travel as extensively as we did, due to family and Temple responsibilities. I concentrated more locally on my carpentry and Priestly duties.

Work was plentiful. I taught our children to love God and obey His commandments. We also taught our sons and daughters to love everyone and not to disrespect anyone. I assured myself what had happened to me as a child would never happen with my children.

Melcha taught the girls domestic skills from an early age. We did not consider ourselves wealthy, but we did not do without, and we maintained a high status amongst our peers. We both made sure all our children would be independent, and humble, advancing into adulthood.

***

Melcha and I were married for over to three decades when she abruptly died from an undocumented illness. I was in the Temple when one of my sons ran to fetch me. My grief overwhelmed me.

"Oh, heavenly Father. How could this happen? Why did this happen? What am I to do now? I still have two young boys to raise. How can I raise them by myself?"

I lamented for days. The love of my life was gone. All but two of our children had started their own families and businesses. Our youngest sons, Judas and James, were still small children. After praying and praying, I resolved to take control and care for my sons. They needed me. My other children graciously offered to help whenever I needed them. For this I was grateful.

***

Several months had passed when I received a message from a couple, Joachim, a High Priest of

King Harrod's court, and his wife, Ann, in the city of Jerusalem, about ninety ·miles south of Nazareth. I had been referred to them by an earlier client from the same area. My memories, good and bad, haunted me. My reasoning to escape my emotional pain and keep my mind busy created an opportunity. My reputation as a carpenter, and a pious man, had preceded me.

Joachim and Ann wished to hire me to craft them a piece of furniture for an upcoming celebration, their daughter, Mary's, first birthday.

I took into consideration that being in King Harrod's province could prove a hazardous venture. Everyone in the region knew of King Herod and his wicked reputation and temper. I was not sure I wanted to subject my sons to this kind of perilous environment, so I left them in the care of their married siblings.

Joachim had become quite financially wealthy and enjoyed many court privileges. I could also use the generous figure that was being offered. I even contemplated a visit with two of my younger brothers, still living in the Bethlehem area. They had reached out, over the years, asking for forgiveness for the way they treated me when we were children.

***

Upon arriving in Jerusalem, I met with Joachim and Ann, and their daughter, Mary, was nearing her first birthday. I presented the plans for the project to their stipulations, and they were accepted.

Mary would often bring me water and meals as I worked. She was such a sweet child. I completed my project, displaying the cabinet to the couple for their approval. Joachim was generous. I thanked him and departed for Bethlehem.

My reunion with my brothers and their families was pleasant, exchanging hugs and tears. Jesse and Asa had both died several years ago. I had long forgiven past transgressions. My brothers coveted their wish that I consider moving closer. However, Nazareth had been my home for many years, and my children, associates, and friends were there. I carried a deep emotional load over losing Melcha for many years.

A MIRACLE

My name is Mary, and this is my beginning as told by the Superioress from the Order, as Ann, my mother, had related it to her. Ann was married to Joachim, a High Priest in King Harrod's court, for several decades. Ann had been barren since their wedding. At her age, her condition was something in which she could no longer endure.

***

One morning, she addressed Joachim. "Joachim, my dear, I am so sorry," she apologized. "I know you wanted an heir, but I have exhausted all avenues. I have consulted with physicians to no avail. I have prayed to The Almighty for decades. I have made offerings and sacrifices to the altar at the Temple. The One above has either not answered or ignored my pleas. All of our friends and family have children, and I am now beyond childbearing years. Why has The Almighty forsaken me and left me barren? What have I done that I must suffer so? Do you feel I have evil within me?"

"Extinguish your fears," Joachim comforted her. "You have done nothing wrong. It is the Lord's will, nothing more. If it were meant to be, it would be. I am content."

"Husband, you are entitled to an heir. You can divorce me, by law, remarry, and achieve the offspring you deserve."

"Ann, my love," he admonished, sternly. "You are my one and only love. I would never entertain any such proposal."

She continued. "Then, perhaps, you could choose to lay with one of the servants, as Abraham once did. We can raise the child as our own. We could sell and send the servant far away after she conceives. No one would ever be the wiser."

Joachim was horrified, increasing the intensity and volume of his voice. "You are suggesting I do what? You are asking me to commit adultery? I would never engage in such an atrocious act, no matter how others have acted in the past, and you know it. I am repelled you could suggest such a calculating idea."

In anger, Joachim stomped out of the house in disbelief.

"Where are you going?" she screamed in tears.
"Out!"

***

Ann was in agony for hours. She felt like she may have lost her husband, regardless of her supportive intensions. Would he ever speak to her again? Had her actions caused a rift in their marriage that was irrecoverable? Where could he have gone? Would he return?

Joachim slipped in late that night and entered the spare sleeping chamber.

Ann cried herself to sleep.

***

The next morning, she found Joachim packing a bag with some clothing and personal essentials.

He turned when she entered the room. "Ann, I am journeying into the wilderness to fast and pray. I don't know how long I will be gone," he announced, obviously still angry from last evening. As he exited, accompanied with his personal servant and two guards for protection, he added, "Upon my return, we will never speak of this again. Do you understand?"

"Oh, yes, my husband, but please do not leave me alone like this. I am so sorry. Can we talk about this?"

Silence was followed by the slamming of the door.

Ann realized the mistake she made. She had never seen him so angry before. She shuttered to think what he was going to say upon his return. Falling to her knees, she prayed, weeping uncontrollably.

"Oh, Great Father, please, forgive me for what I have done. I never intended to alienate Joachim. I pray I have not lost the love of my life because of my unimaginable solution. Oh, Great Father, please, help me."

***

That evening, Ann was still grieving over their argument. The sun was dipping into the western sky. Shadows were gliding over the garden foliage like a fog engulfing a small pond. Enjoying the beautiful fragrance of rose petals, Ann was meditating, alone.

Ann thought it strange when the familiar songs regional birds were singing ceased. A gentle breeze, gently shifting her silk robes, ended. A movement caught her eye as a mist appeared and a human form began to materialize.

An Angel adorning shoulder-length hair and garbed in a billowing white robe was surrounded by a blinding, glowing light. He appeared before her and spoke.

"Ann, be not afraid. I am the Archangel Gabriel; God has heard your prayers and I have divine news. You are to have a daughter and you will name her Mary. There is only one condition, to keep this child from sin and evil, you are required to surrender Mary to the Order of Temple Virgins after her third birthday, where she will be safe from impending harm."

"Oh, I thank you with all my heart!" Ann replied. "I did not think this was possible at my age. The Lord has heard our prayers after all. But why must we surrender her to the Order?" However, when she perused her surroundings, Gabriel had already disappeared.

Ann was so excited about the revelation, but she was also distressed about how Joachim departed; however, she decided she was no longer dwelling upon it.

***

Weeks later, Joachim returned, and she met him at the door.

"Welcome home, Joachim. I was so worried. Are you all right? Did you have a religious experience during your cleansing, my husband?" she asked with a smile on her face.

Joachim looking irritated, replied, "No, I did not. After these forty days, I was eaten alive by insects, exhausted, starving, and in dire need of a bath. Even the servants camped at a distance." Then noticing her whimsical expression, he said, "I am no mood to argue anymore. Why are you asking, and what are you grinning about?" he asked, annoyed.

She repressed from bursting as she eagerly announced, "Well," she paused then smiled and added, "I did, and you are going to be a papa."

"I'm what?" he asked with a stunned facial expression.

Ann then conveyed to him about her heavenly visit, the announcement, and the condition attached.

Neither of them could comprehend why there was a condition but accepted it as the Lord's will.

They knew and accepted that The Almighty knows all but does not always convey the reasoning.

***

Over the next few months, Ann was buzzing around like a bee moving from flower to flower, preparing for their daughter's arrival. They had the spare bedroom transformed into a nursery and furnished.

The pregnancy sickness prevented her from keeping little nourishment down for weeks. Her personal servant carried a bowl, partially filled or empty, at all times.

***

As the months progressed and I increased in size, and she became more miserable, as it came closer to her time. The first moment she felt a kick, Ann relayed it felt like it was coming through her stomach wall. It scared her. Ann's servant midwife assured her it was normal.

***

Ann's labor lasted for over eighteen hours. She had never experienced such pain in her entire life. She knew death was just around the corner.

When Mary was born, all the previous discomfort was forgotten. It was the most glorious day of their lives. Joachim had a tear in his eye, but he would never admit it.

***

On the eighth day after Mary was born, the Brit Banot ceremony was held at the Temple, announcing her name.

Ann knew Mary was a gifted child from infancy. She began walking at six months and talking in full sentences at eleven months. For Mary's first birthday, a carpenter was retained from Nazareth to build a special cabinet.

Mary loved bringing him refreshments while he worked. A celebration banquet, including fellow High Priests and friends, was held in their home.

To their chagrin, after Mary's third birthday, they obeyed The Almighty's condition, and relinquished Mary to the Order.

JOSEPH MEETS MARY

A decade later, I was attending to my duties in the Temple, when I accepted an announcement by messenger from the Order of the Temple Virgins, near Jerusalem.

"Hear Ye, Hear Ye. To all eligible males from the Twelve Tribes of Judah, from this day forward, the Order of Temple Virgins is seeking a benefactor and betrothal to a young maiden who has become of age. All single interested candidates, please submit your name and qualifying credentials. An honorary candidate will be selected, and the announcement will be forthcoming. The maiden's personal history can be obtained by the nominated applicant upon request. After a period of one year, the unity in marriage can be finalized."

Normally, I would not pay any attention to these announcements, as they do occur occasionally. Since Melcha's passing. I had not thought about another woman.

***

I mentioned the announcement to my family one evening during dinner, and they all agreed enough time had passed. It was time to move on; I deserved to be happy. I was also aware that James and Judas, as young as they were, needed a mother figure in their lives, other than their sisters. I submitted my name and credentials then dispatched them by messenger, to the Order. I thought that was the last time I would hear of this until the news of a selected contender had been announced I learned later, there were eleven others that had applied.

***

A few months had passed, and I received an official proclamation from the Order.

"Joseph, from the House of David, you have been selected as the benefactor to the young maiden named Mary. Please, travel at your earliest convenience, to Order of the Temple Virgins to meet and officially become Mary's guardian, accepting all responsibilities forthwith. All known pertinent information will be made available to you, at your request, upon your arrival."

***

After securing care for the boys, I arrived at the Order a month later and I met with the Superioress.

"Very little is known about Mary," the Superioress began after our initial introductions. "I will share what I know. I met her parents, Joachim and Ann; they were from Jerusalem, and Mary was brought to us in secretly," the Superioress relayed to me.

"Why do those names sound familiar?" I asked myself.

"Joachim was a one of King Harrod's High Priests."

Then, it clicked.

"Now I remember," Joseph interrupted. "I was hired to design and build a cabinet for them to celebrate their daughter's first birthday celebration. It's been at least ten years ago."

"The little girl brought me water and some meals. Such a sweet child, I seem to recollect."

"Well, isn't that intriguing?" the Superioress whispered.

The Superioress expanded, "I remember watching Mary dance on the third step of the alter in glee, to everyone's amazement upon their arrival. After contributing a sizable donation, I never saw Mary's parents again. All legal connection to her parents was severed once the Order took custody, for her own protection. How or why her parents lost favor with King Harrod and were executed by his soldiers is unclear. I heard all properties and assets were confiscated. No one outside of the Order had knowledge of Mary's whereabouts."

Superioress divulged information inside the Order about Mary, including her religious and domestic training and duties.

"Mary," one of our high priests addressed Mary when she was ten, 'we are taking you into an undisclosed area in the wilderness to be alone for a full day and night. When we return, and you are unharmed, that will be proof of your purity.'

"The Order sisters had advised Mary this would happen, and she was prepared. Mary was taken to a distant location into the countryside. This was an area known for inhabiting wildlife, and she was placed. Interestingly enough, Mary disclosed she was never frightened. I don't know why, but she knew she would be safe.

"The next day, the Priests and their guards returned and found her surrounded by wild animals of different species and sizes, lying all about, protecting her. The clerical ensemble had never seen anything like it. When they approached, the animals scattered, and she was proclaimed to be pure of heart and soul.

"Mary," I addressed her a couple of years later, 'you are nearing the age for betrothal. You have no known family. Therefore, we are sending a notice to all the heads of the twelve tribes of Judah, announcing your availability. We will select the best candidate, from those who respond, to be your betrothal protector.'

"Yes, Superioress," Mary had answered. 'I understand. I know I cannot remain here forever. Everyone here has been so kind. You have all trained me well, and I am ready. I know you have only my best interest at heart. I will be forever grateful. The Archangel Gabriel appeared to the me, while I was in prayer for guidance.'

"I am the Archangel, Gabriel. I am here to bring a command from God. The man you will choose for the betrothal of Mary is Joseph, from the house of David in Nazareth. Heed and obey the Word of our Lord."

"The apparition, for me, was twofold," she told me. "I felt blessed and honored, receiving a rare apparition and was frightened at the same time. I took the message to heart. The appearance of the elimination process proceeded as planned, taking a few months. We sent you the notification as the selectee."

The Superioress told me an announcement would be posted, making it official.

We said our goodbyes to the Superioress and the sisters and then departed with Mary's chaperone, Ruth.

***

Shortly after we arrived home, I was called away, on business, some distance away. I had not expected to be gone long. However, I was gone for over two years. Nearby friends and family gave Mary and the boys the support when needed. I was confident that she and the boys were quite safe, capable, and happy.

THE ANNUNCIATION

Joseph had been gone for close to two years. Periodically, we would receive progress reports, but nothing that indicated when Joseph would be returning home. I was taking a daily trip to the community well, with Ruth, to fetch some water. House buckets were hanging from the yokes around our necks, when I heard a voice, more like a whisper, calling my name.

"Mary."

"Yes, Ruth," I asked?

Ruth turned and replied with a confused look on her face, "I didn't say anything."

My name was called again.

"Mary."

"Hello," I replied, turning around in the direction from whence the voice came. "Is there someone there?" I inquired, hesitating for a minute and then pondered. "That's odd," I said to myself. Ruth had walked ahead and had not heard me the second time. Shaking my head, thinking I had lost my mind, I brushed it off.

Ruth and I trekked back to the house. I had chores to do and supper to prepare. I had no time for this nonsense. I had two growing boys to feed.

***

That evening, I was working by candlelight. It created shadows, emulating my movements, dancing across the walls in the room. I was finishing spinning thread for my Temple veil in preparation for Joseph and my marriage ceremony upon his return. The boys and Ruth were fast asleep on their mats. A light quickly encased the room, and an angel appeared.

"Mary, I am the Archangel Gabriel. The Lord be With You. Calm yourself, for I have a message from The Almighty. You are with Child, God's Son, the Messiah."

I withdrew in fear and then asked. "With what? How, can this be?" I gasped in horror, knowing the implications. "By all that is holy, I am a virgin."

"This is God's present to you. He has placed the Holy Spirit within you. This will be no ordinary child, for He is the Lord's Son. He will be a Leader of men and will be loved. You will be worshipped and adored for many a millennium. Your cousin, Elizabeth, in the town of Beth Hakerem, near Jerusalem, is with child, a boy, to be named John. John is to pave the way for the Messiah. She is almost six months along, and Elizabeth needs you. Go now and be of assistance."

The room went back to normal, and Gabriel was gone. I was not familiar with Elizabeth, knowing nothing of her or of her having a baby almost a hundred miles from here. Much less, assisting someone in childbirth. A calming feeling covered me, like a silk garment slowly gliding over my being. I was still frightened, but obeying God's Word, I said aloud, "The Almighty's will be done."

"I sat in silence for a few minutes, shaking. Eventually, I accepted what I had just experienced, and heeding the angel's message, I prepared to leave quickly.

Joseph's family, a little confused, helped and made Ruth and my upcoming journey arrangements.

I left the boys with them. Here I am, not yet officially married, to an older established Priest and artisan and pregnant. I knew unmarried pregnant girls were not looked upon with kindness. Even though I did not show, it would only be a matter of time before people would notice. Prejudged fallen women could be subjected to death by stoning, per Hebrew law. I was so afraid.

***

The trek to Beth Hakerem was not a particularly pleasant trip, accompanying the caravan comprised of merchants and fellow travelers. Ruth and I walked, as we had no other transportation, but we were young and strong. The road was not much more than a glorified goat path, full of rocks and holes. We had to avoid getting our feet trapped and twisting an ankle. Dodging camel and equine droppings became a skillful daily task.

We stopped to camp for the night whenever there was a large enough area for us all.

Communal tents were erected, only when it rained. Fires were started with collected wood or dried animal
dung, and our individual evening meals were prepared from what we packed. If we were
lucky to be near fir trees, softer bedding was a comfort. If not, we made the best we could on
very hard, rocky ground, and a blanket.

I tried to make conversation, but friendships among strangers was habitually avoided. I
approached a woman dressed in a flowing colorful skirt and blouse and wearing a hajib. I was
hoping she could speak Hebrew.

"Shalom, my name is Mary, and this is my companion, Ruth," I greeted her. "We have
little travel experience and would like some advice."

"My advice to you is not to ask too many questions," the woman curtly answered with
an Arabic accent. She continued, "Road travel is not pleasant, and stranger associations do not
last for obvious reasons. No one will steal from you and you do not steal from anyone else. Keep to yourselves and keep up. This way, you will make your destination safely." Then, she walked away.

"Well, that was abrupt," Ruth observed.

"I guess, with the dangers of the times," Mary alleged, "avoiding casual friends makes
sense because they do not last. Most will never see each other again."

"Okay, I can see that," Ruth agreed.

***

We arrived at the outskirts of Jerusalem, about three miles north of Beth Hakerem after almost two weeks of traveling.

"Excuse me," I asked a shop owner upon entering town. "Could you direct me to the home of Zachariah and Elizabeth?"

"They live in the last house on the right at the end of this street," he replied. "You should be there in about ten minutes. Shalom."

"Thank you," I responded.

Ruth and I walked until we reached the last home, as directed.

I knocked on the door, and a woman, obviously very pregnant, wearing a well-worn cotton gown, answered.

"Shalom," I greeted her. "Would you be Elizabeth? I am your cousin. Mary, and I am here to help you and your baby."

Elizabeth grabbed her stomach and said in glee, "Shalom, I am so happy to meet you, Mary. I see you are with child, as well."

I seemed surprised that Elizabeth knew, since I displayed no physical sign.

"I just felt my baby, John, jump for joy when I opened the door. I have never felt this reaction before. Your baby must be Someone special."

"Indeed, He shall be."

Turning to Ruth, I introduced her to Elizabeth. "Elizabeth, this is Ruth, my companion."

"Welcome, Ruth, make yourself at home."

MY TRIP HOME

I was told of Mary's trip to her cousins by way of a mutual friend. Finishing my last project, I made my way to Beth Hakerem. I decided that I had been away long enough.

I stopped for the night at the outskirts of Beth Hakerem. I did not want to intrude this late in the evening. I had settled down for the night when I heard footsteps and voices approaching.

"Who is out there?" I yelled into the night beyond my campfire. I listened as I heard I assumed thieves shuffling around in the darkness. I had the good fortune to hide a couple of coin bags in the sand near my bedroll. I kept those aside as a precautionary measure. The warning of distinct clanging of metal weapons sounded and then a deep voice rang out.

"Stay where you are and the only thing you will lose is your belongings. Do not attempt to follow us," the threatening voice declared.

Fearing for my life, I thought it was in my best interest to obey. They stealthily disappeared into the darkness. Almost all I had earned, some gifts I was bringing back, and most of my personal belongings, were lost, including my pack animal. I was heartbroken, but thinking of Mary and the boys brightened my objective. Material things could be replaced, my life could not.

***

Entering Beth Hakerem, I inquired about the location of Zachariah and Elizabeth's home from a resident I met along the road.

I knocked on the door, and Mary answered. I cannot explain the astonishing surprise on my face finding her visibly showing. I believe our facial expressions spoke volumes.

Mary suggested we go for a walk and talk.

"Joseph, this is not as it appears." Looking down at her stomach, she continued, in panic mode. "Well, it is, but I can explain." Mary then began to replay her stage of events. "As the Lord is my witness, this is the truth, Joseph."

Mary told me about home life with the boys and the appearance of the Archangel Gabriel. She told me about Gabriel's message and that we would name the male child, Jesus, and He was The Almighty's Son and would be a Leader of men. Then, she told me about Gabriel telling her about Elizabeth, going to help her with her child on the way.

"That's why I am here. You must believe me," Mary pleaded, weeping.

I peered at her with a dubious look, shook my head, and declared. "Mary, I, uh, need some time alone to take this in. Please, excuse me."

With that, I walked away to contemplate my next move.

Mary ran back into the house, crying uncontrollably. She had confided in Elizabeth, knowing her experience.

Elizabeth comforted her as best she could.

"Oh, Elizabeth, what will happen to me now? Will Joseph accept all this, or will he have me stoned as Jewish law allows?"

***

I went back the next day and took Mary aside with every intention of undergoing the most logical strategy for this most sensitive situation.

"Mary, I love you, and you will never know how beholden I am to you caring for my boys and giving them a wonderful homelife during my long, unexpected absence. I will be eternally grateful. However, what you are trying to convince me to believe, even as a devoted Temple priest, is beyond my comprehension. I know Jewish law and the penalty of this type of situation and how it has been traditionally handled," I confided in Mary after my sleepless night of considering all possibilities.

"From what you have endeavored to explain, this situation is not traditional. I will not allow a stoning to happen, so this is what I will do. I will still marry you, in a private ceremony. We will begin our journey home as soon as Elizabeth's baby is born. No

45

one at home knows when I arrived here or when we married. Nor will anyone learn that from me.

"As soon as your child is born, we will seek a quiet secretive divorce. I will supply you a home and will covertly continue to support you and your Child, but in the eyes of the public, we will
have parted ways. That is the best solution I can devise under the circumstances."

I concluded my condition of terms and walked away, ignoring her pleas to come back and reconsider.

***

I again spent the night alone. As I lay sleeping, restlessly, I experienced an apparition of my own when Gabriel appeared to me in a dream.

"Joseph, Joseph, awaken."

"Uh, what? Who's there? What do you want? You've taken all I have. Leave me alone.
Wait a minute, how do you know my name?"

"Joseph, I am the Archangel Gabriel, and I bring good news. Everything Mary told you is true. I appeared to Mary and told her she was carrying the Lord's Son, Jesus. I also told her about Elizabeth and that she needed Mary's help. Go forth in peace knowing this. Comfort Mary in her strife. Love and care for Mary her for the rest of your days."

***

I awoke the next morning, abruptly sitting up in bed, and remembering what I had told Mary last evening and my apparition with the Angel.

"What have I done?" I shouted aloud to myself.

***

I quickly returned to Zachariah and Elizabeth's home and knocked.

Mary answered the door. Her eyes swollen and tears running down her face from being despondent all night.

I instantly took her into my arms. "Mary, say nothing. Please, forgive me for doubting you. Gabriel visited me last night in a dream and told me everything. Forget everything I said last night, except the part about marrying you today. I would be honored to marry you, if you will still have me. Today is a new day and the beginning of our life together as husband and wife. I will love and care for you and our child as long as I live."

Listening to what I said, Mary replied. "Oh, Joseph; our child." Mary caught my meaning. Her face shinned with a look of relief and happiness. "I am elated to marry you and begin our wonderful and glorious life together."

***

Our wedding happened that same day by a priest arranged by Zachariah in a private ceremony, with Elizabeth and Zachariah in attendance; both serving as witnesses. The voyage home to Nazareth commenced after the birth of John. Zachariah's voice returned, as promised, immediately after. We brought back Ruth to her Order on our way, as her services were no longer required.

ROMAN CENSUS

Mary and I reached home in Nazareth, much to the delight of our family and friends. James and Judas were the first to see us coming and ran down the path to greet us.

"Oh, Papa, we are so happy you are home, we missed you so much!" James and Judas shouted in unison.

"You, too, Mary," James, the youngest, said, giving her a hug. "Did you get bigger? My arms cannot reach around like they used to," he observed.

"James, that's rude," I scolded him, trying to suppress a grin.

"That's fine." Mary acknowledged James's observance.

"You are correct, James; you and Judas are going to have a little brother," I explained.

"Really?" both brothers yelled in excitement. "How wonderful; when?"

"In about six months from now. I am happy you are pleased," Mary said, relieved at their acceptance.

"But, aren't you supposed to be married, or something, before you have a baby?" Judas inquired.

"We are married, Judas," Papa informed him. "We married in Beth Hakerem after I joined Mary at her cousin, Elizabeth's. Zachariah's associate Priest performed the ceremony."

James's facial expression exploded with glee at a double surprise. "Oh, Papa and Mary, married and having a baby, what wonderful news. Can we have a party to celebrate?"

"As soon as possible," we both agreed, laughing. "Can we unpack and rest first?"

***

An announcement was made and a party was held, a week later, in our honor. A spectacular buffet celebration was enjoyed by all. There was music and dancing. Open pit lamb with vegetables were served, along with various fruit juice sweetened breads. Both family and friends were in attendance.

***

A few months went by, I kept busy with my duties as a priest and as a carpenter. Mary was coming close to term when the Roman decree was declared for a tax required census. All family heads were obligated to return to the city of their birth to resister.

"Mary, I have to travel to Bethlehem to register our family for the Roman Census. I should not be gone more than a month or so. I pleaded with our local Roman representative to postpone my going because of your condition, but it was denied. You will be fine here with family and friends until my return."

"No, Joseph, although my time is near, we will be together when our son arrives," Mary answered.

"But Mary, it is a long, strenuous trip. I am certain the city will be crowded, and it will be difficult to find lodging for one traveler, much less a couple. Besides, in your condition, you should not be making such a journey. I strongly feel it would be in your best interest to remain here," Joseph reasoned.

"Joseph, my love, we were separated before for a period of over two years. I promised myself that would never happen again. So, please, take me with you, and we will deal with whatever comes our way," Mary pleaded. "Besides, it will give me an opportunity to meet your brothers and their families."

I knew whatever argument I could produce would not matter. The trip was going include both of us. I conceded, and Mary prepared double rations for our journey. I purchased a donkey for Mary to ride, led by me, to make her trek more comfortable and carry our possessions. Horses were too expensive, so I opted for a cheaper and calmer and surefooted donkey.

We departed the next morning after saying our goodbyes to family, leaving the boys with them.

***

We stopped in the foothills of Mt. Gilboa by the river Jordan our first night.

Mary started a fire from dead dry limbs I had gathered. She fixed our meal while I set up camp.

We talked and discussed our future while we starred at the stars in the evening sky. I was glad Mary was convincing in accompanying me. I was enjoying the companionship.

Mary had such an eloquent talent in her storytelling recalling our time apart.

"What is the matter, boys?" Mary asked, finding them in distress. They were crying and obviously depressed, crouching in a corner of the house, together. She wished to help, if she could, even though she was not that many years older than they.

"We miss Mama," the boys told her. "We miss her so," they lamented, tears streaming down their faces.

"Can you tell me about her so I can know her better?" Mary asked and then smiled.

They did.

When they finished, Mary assured both brothers. "Your mother is now in a beautiful place, with The One above, along with past family members and friends."

I comforted them. "You both will see her again, but not in this world. She is looking down on you both and smiling. Be at peace in knowing that." I placed my hands on both of their heads and bowed my head and offering a blessing.

A tranquil feeling enveloped over the boys, and their deep feelings of sorrow dissipated.

"You are so good for them, Mary. They both love you very much," I acknowledged their relationship and her skill as a surrogate mother. "I noticed that even in the short time I was home."

Mary told me of hers and Ruth's journey to Elizabeth's. "As a young maiden, I could not, travel alone, for many obvious reasons. I had confided in Ruth, who accompanied me. Your older son's arranged passage with a caravan travelling to Jerusalem, after informing them about Elizabeth's condition. I did not reveal that I had not known about Elizabeth. I thought it prudent not to. Travelling with an established caravan would provide safety in numbers. I learned and was assured, by some of our village women, that women traveling in caravans stuck together and protected each other. This ninety-plus mile journey would be long and arduous. I prayed it would be a safe trip."

Mary continued, "We camped out every night. Our days were sunny, but not exceedingly hot. Our nights were brisk, but I learned how to build a campfire, which kept Ruth and I comfortable. We were aware of the possible hazards that we could face, like bandits, harsh weather, and wild animals, but we experienced very few. There were community tents erected just in case of bad weather. I had the feeling we had an invisible cloak sheathing us."

When we arrived on the outskirts of Jerusalem, we left the caravan and walked for about three miles to the town of Beth Hakerem.

Addressing a local vender, Mary asked, "Shalom, would you direct us to the home of Zachariah and Elizabeth, please?"

"Shalom, of course; it is the last house on the right past town. Visiting, are we?" he replied.

"Yes," Mary answered. "Elizabeth is my cousin."

"Have a nice visit."

"Thank you."

***

We were greeted by Elizabeth and Zachariah upon arriving at their home. Zachariah was mute, something I learned why later, so he could only nod a greeting.

Elizabeth gasped and cupped her stomach in happiness. "I just felt my baby move like he was jumping for joy. It is like he knows who you are and who you are carrying. Blessed are you and blessed is the fruit of thy womb."

I was astonished. How could she know?

We had many long evening talks.

Elizabeth shared, "Zacharias and I had been married for many decades, and I had

54

been barren, like Ann and Sarah, as told in the Torah scriptures. Both had seen six decades pass. Zacharias, a temple Priest was taking his turn assignment in the temple to burn incense. This was an honored duty that only happened once in a lifetime. This chamber of the temple could only be entered, by a selected Priest, alone. As Zachariah worked, a mist appeared. A man materialized on Zacharia's right side. It unnerved Zachariah because this was a strictly solidary assignment.

"Do not be afraid, Zacharias," Gabriel, the angel assured him, placing his hand on Zacharias's shoulder." I am the Archangel Gabriel. I am here with a message from God, to inform you that Elizabeth will have a son, and you will call him John. John will be the preempt profit to the Messiah. John will never partake of the vine, and he will be filled with the Holy Spirit. His life will be dedicated to the Lord's service."*

"Zacharia questioned Gabriel, saying, 'Elizabeth is beyond her childbearing years, how can this be?'

"I am God's messenger!" roared Gabriel, forcing Zacharia to take a step back in fear and fall to his knees. *"You dare to commit an offense to The Almighty by doubting His Word. From this moment on, until the day your son is born, you will be silenced. Now go and be with your wife, Elizabeth."*

"In an instant, he vanished along with the mist."

"Zacharia shook with fear for several minutes. He finished his duties and exited the holy chamber. Zacharia first realized he had lost his speech outside the temple. People took notice he could not respond when spoken to, and they suspected something had happened inside the temple.

"Zacharia tried his best to relate his experience in a silent, panicked attempt of a response and then attempted hand jesters to no avail. How could he perform his duties as a Priest as a mute? Zachariah returned home and was informed Elizabeth simultaneously had experienced a similar visit. She had wisely not questioned Gabriel and believed her husband and mourned his chastisement. It was difficult for him to explain in sign, but he got his point across. Within months, Elizabeth began showing the signs of being with child and slipped into seclusion."

"As you now know, Elizabeth had a son, John. Immediately after, Zachariah regained his voice, as Gabriel had foretold," Mary finished.

I was in awe. What a divine time Mary had experienced, as well as Zachariah and Elizabeth.

Mary had concluded and said, "Enough about me, tell me about your travels, Joseph."

"Nothing as exciting as what you experienced," I answered. "Every time I finished one project, three more would spring up, as I stated in the letters I sent. I had little time to do anything else. I did think about you and the boys, every night when I retired. I learned of your travelling to Beth Hakerem from a letter from my son but not why. I decided I had been gone long enough and I was going to join you there. I did make a profitable sum after being gone for so long. Unfortunately, I was robbed on my way to Elizabeth's and barely got away with my life. I wisely managed to hide a couple bags they did not find. I am still happy I came. I missed you all so very much."

"We, as well," Mary agreed. "We were happy to have you home again."

***

Every morning, I detected the evidence of different types of large wildlife that had bedded down just beyond our camp's perimeter, every night, encircling us. However, they were gone by early morning. I got the feeling they were there to protect us. When I mentioned it to Mary, she appeared composed. Then, I recalled about the Superioress' accounting during Mary's purity ritual. Amazing.

BETHLEHEM

Our journey took us well over three weeks, partially due to Mary's frequent resting stops. We arrived in Jerusalem one morning and spent a few hours visiting the temple then traveled on to Bethlehem that afternoon. It had grown since I had been there last.

We stopped by both brothers', hoping for lodging, only to find they were full with other guests.

"We are sorry we cannot accommodate you. My wife's parents are here," both brothers apologized. "Had we known; we could have accommodated you both. However, there are two inns in town. Hopefully, you can find a room there."

"Thanks, anyway, we will try that," I replied. I was disappointed, but I understood the circumstances.

***

Late in the evening, we arrived at the first inn, resting at the edge of Bethlehem, but we were told they had no vacancies.

"I am sorry," the proprietor explained. "We are full. You might try the inn at the other end of town. It is owned and managed by James, Ruth and their son, Lacob. Ruth is an amazing cook, and a midwife," he said, having noticed Mary's condition. "I understand they have a young servant, Frieda, helping out, as well. Their inn is larger, and with people coming and going because of the census, hopefully they will be able to accommodate you. Good luck in your search."

It was late.

Darkness had descended with only flickering streetlights and home illuminations visible. We made our way down the main street of Bethlehem, moving past closed businesses, a blacksmith's shop, and then small cramped rowhouse type homes, all sharing at least one interior wall.

The street was vacant, except for a few stragglers and a some packs of barking dogs that roamed around, searching for food. If a dog, snapping at the heels of our donkey came too close, our donkey kicked out, sometimes connecting and then scattering them howling off into the night in pain.

***

At long last, we came upon the inn's sign shingle, hanging from a board, attached to a lamp post. I knocked on the door, praying they had a room. Mary was getting tired, and I knew the donkey was exhausted.

"Please, Your Almighty," I prayed, "please let them have a room for us; anywhere out of the weather will do."

House of David is a prequel to Charles' first book, *Inn's Side.*

Author Charles 'Chuck' Carson, and his wife Pat live on a small farm in White Mills, KY. He is a father and grandfather and a member of The Bards Corner Writer's Group. He has a BS from Urbana University and is a USPS retiree. Besides writing he enjoys woodworking, gardening, painting, photography and music.

Charles is also the author of *Inn's Side* and coming soon, *We're Going Where?* He has been featured in the *Compass Magazine* from the Daniel Boone Society.

Made in the USA
Columbia, SC
18 January 2022

54390452R00039